Everyone's Moon

by Karen Anderson Moushon
Illustrated by Ethan Wagner

Copyright © 2024 Karen Anderson Moushon.

All rights reserved. No part of this book may be used or reproduced by any means, graphic, electronic, or mechanical, including photocopying, recording, taping or by any information storage retrieval system without the written permission of the author except in the case of brief quotations embodied in critical articles and reviews.

Archway Publishing books may be ordered through booksellers or by contacting:

Archway Publishing
1663 Liberty Drive
Bloomington, IN 47403
www.archwaypublishing.com
844-669-3957

Because of the dynamic nature of the Internet, any web addresses or links contained in this book may have changed since publication and may no longer be valid. The views expressed in this work are solely those of the author and do not necessarily reflect the views of the publisher, and the publisher hereby disclaims any responsibility for them.

Any people depicted in stock imagery provided by Getty Images are models, and such images are being used for illustrative purposes only. Certain stock imagery © Getty Images.

Interior Image Credit: Ethan Wagner

ISBN: 978-1-6657-5919-9 (sc)
ISBN: 978-1-6657-5918-2 (hc)
ISBN: 978-1-6657-5917-5 (e)

Library of Congress Control Number: 2024907794

Print information available on the last page.

Archway Publishing rev. date: 06/28/2024

Written with love for my grands and greats:

Landon and Lauren
David and Kai
Becket and Jude
Kaysen and Aspen
Tate
Milo
Jett

And, thank you, Amanda & Katie

At the end of the day when the sun's work is through
and the sky's golden pinks turn to shades of dark blue,

It's everyone's moon, and it climbs up to glow
over all of us here in the big world below.
All of earth's creatures have one moon to share
that glimmers and glows in the night sky up there.

We all get to watch it rise up in the night,
suspended in midair until morning's light,
lighting the darkness with its golden hue
while together, wherever, we take in the view.

We marvel at how it can be seen from here,
so far away yet so wonderfully clear.

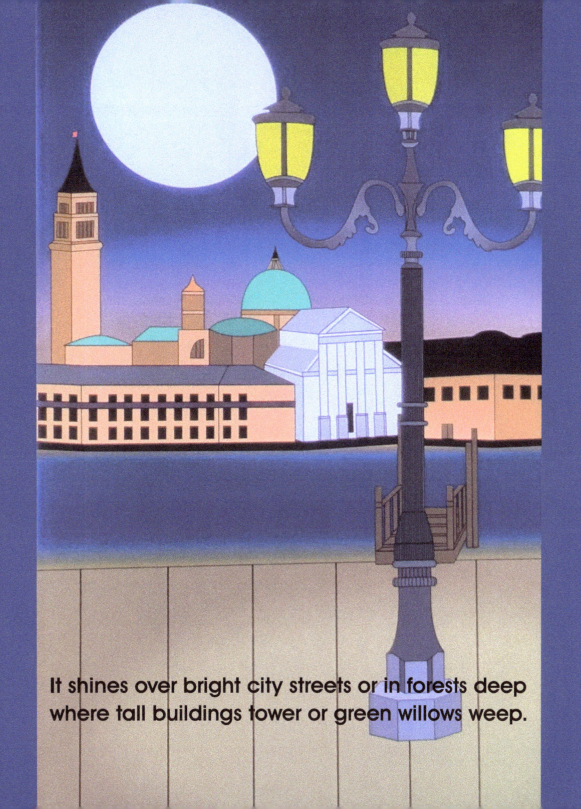

It shines over bright city streets or in forests deep where tall buildings tower or green willows weep.

Whether silent night owl or busy raccoon,
all bask in the rays of the shimmering moon.

No one can buy it or lock it away.
It's there for us all at the end of each day.

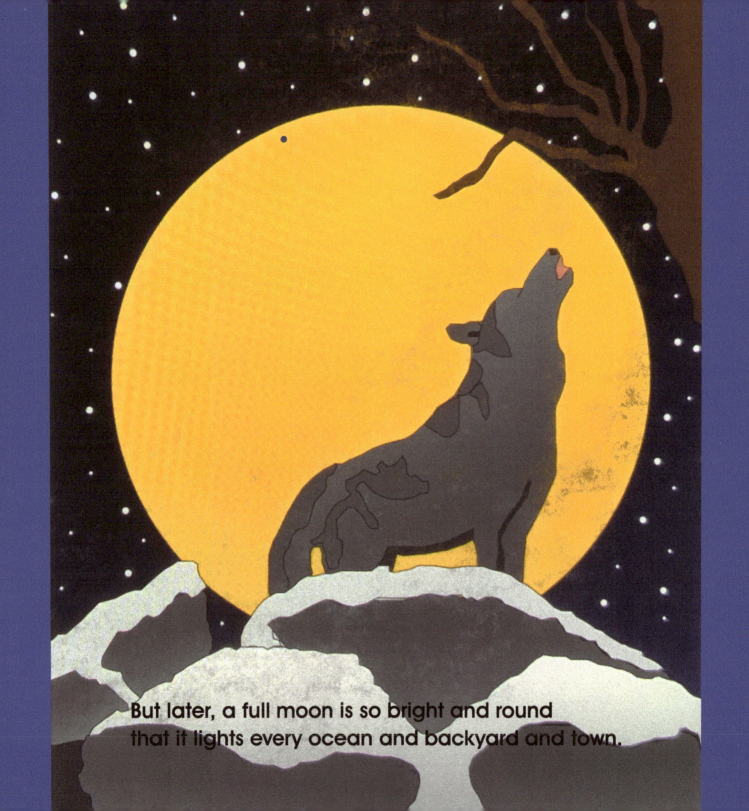

But later, a full moon is so bright and round
that it lights every ocean and backyard and town.

No matter how different or how far apart,
we share the same view of one moon after dark.

it's for all of us, everywhere, down here below.